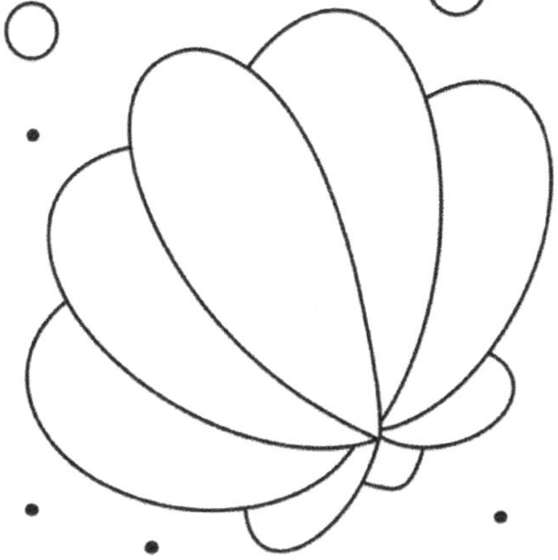

This book belongs to:

ISBN: 9798544323358

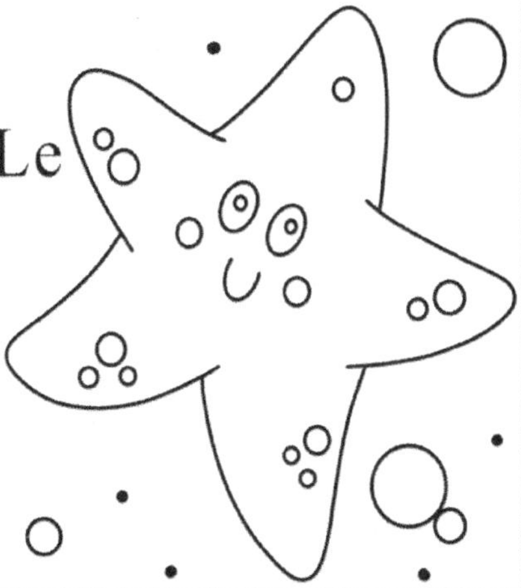

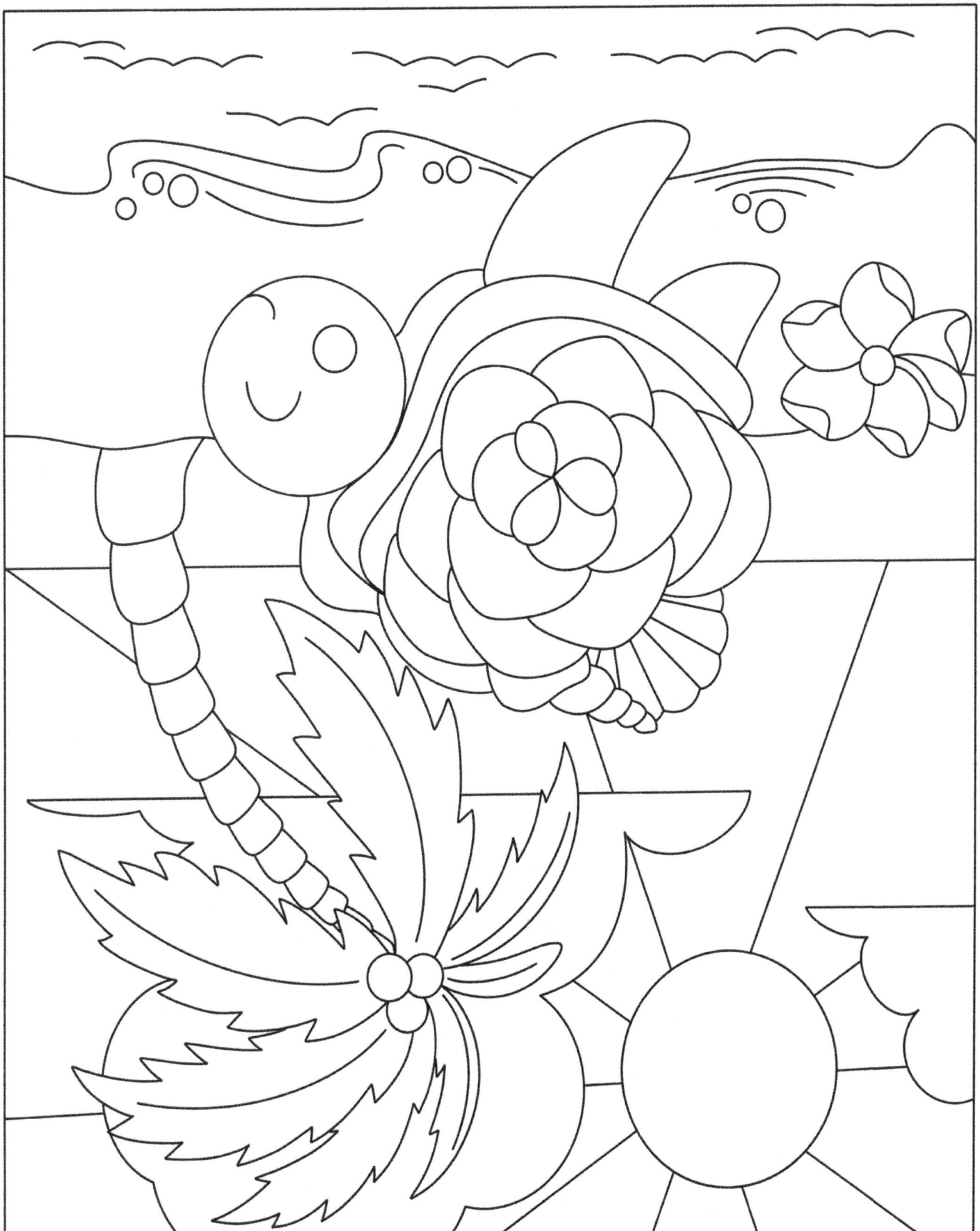

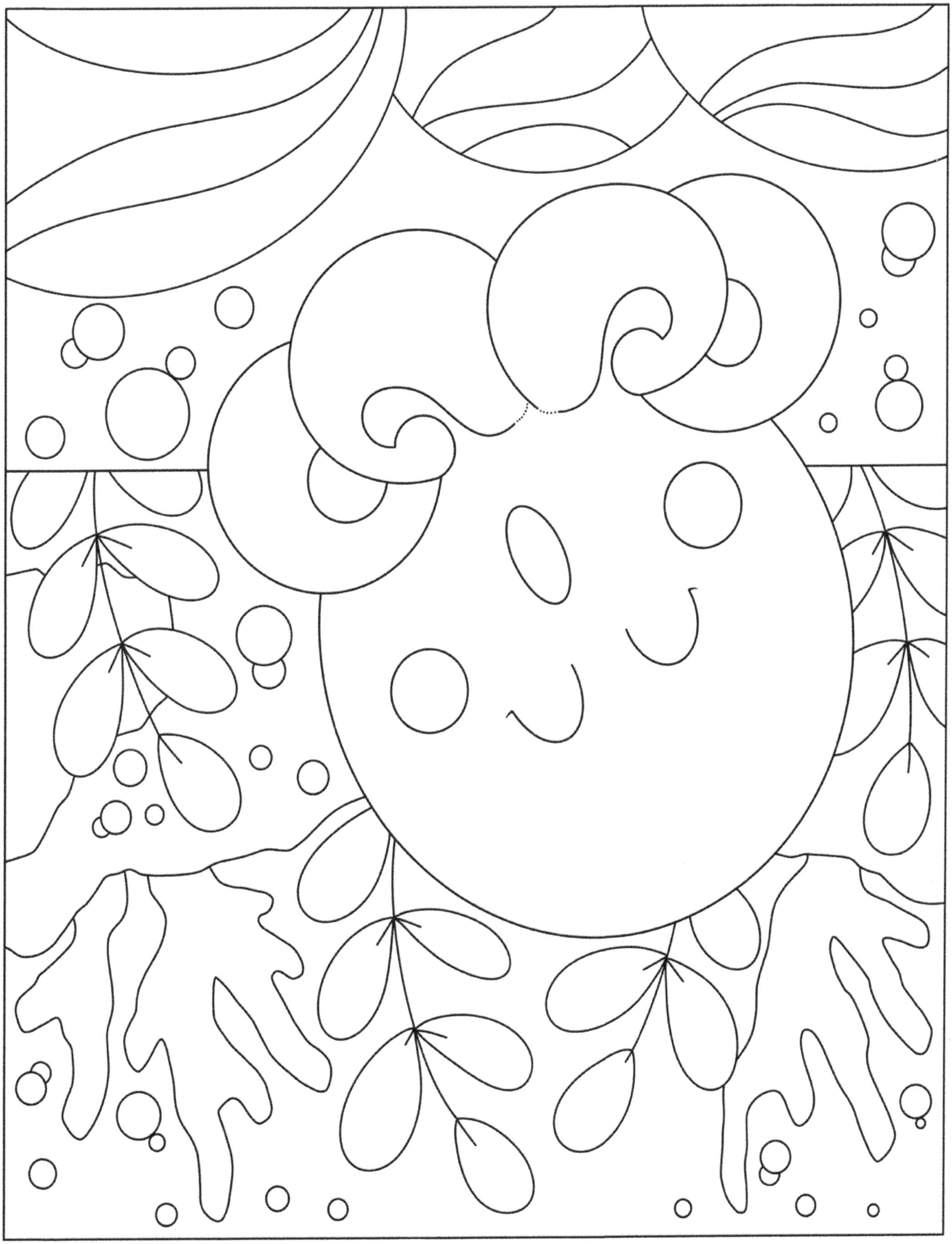

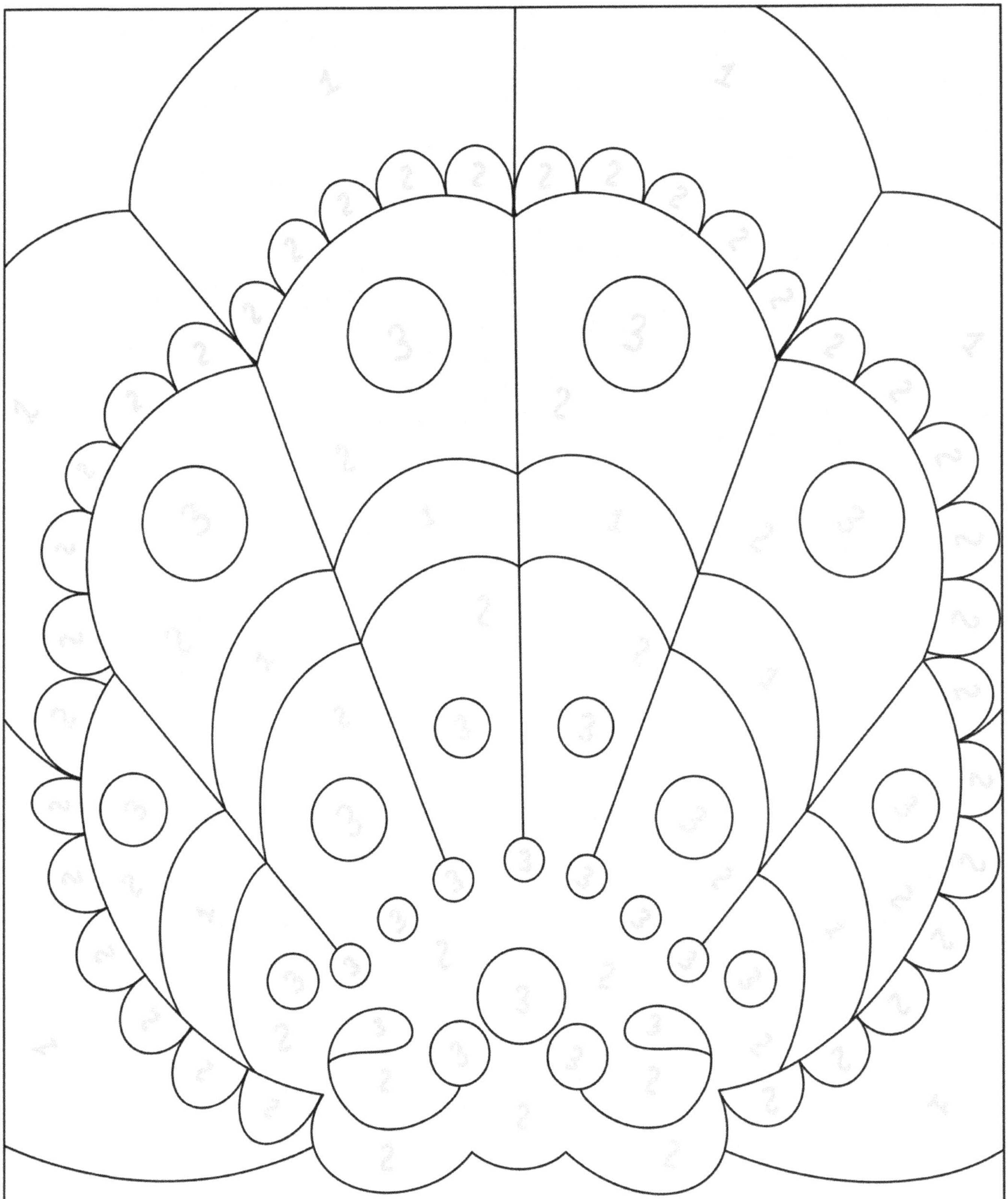

1 Blue   2 Purple   3 Yellow

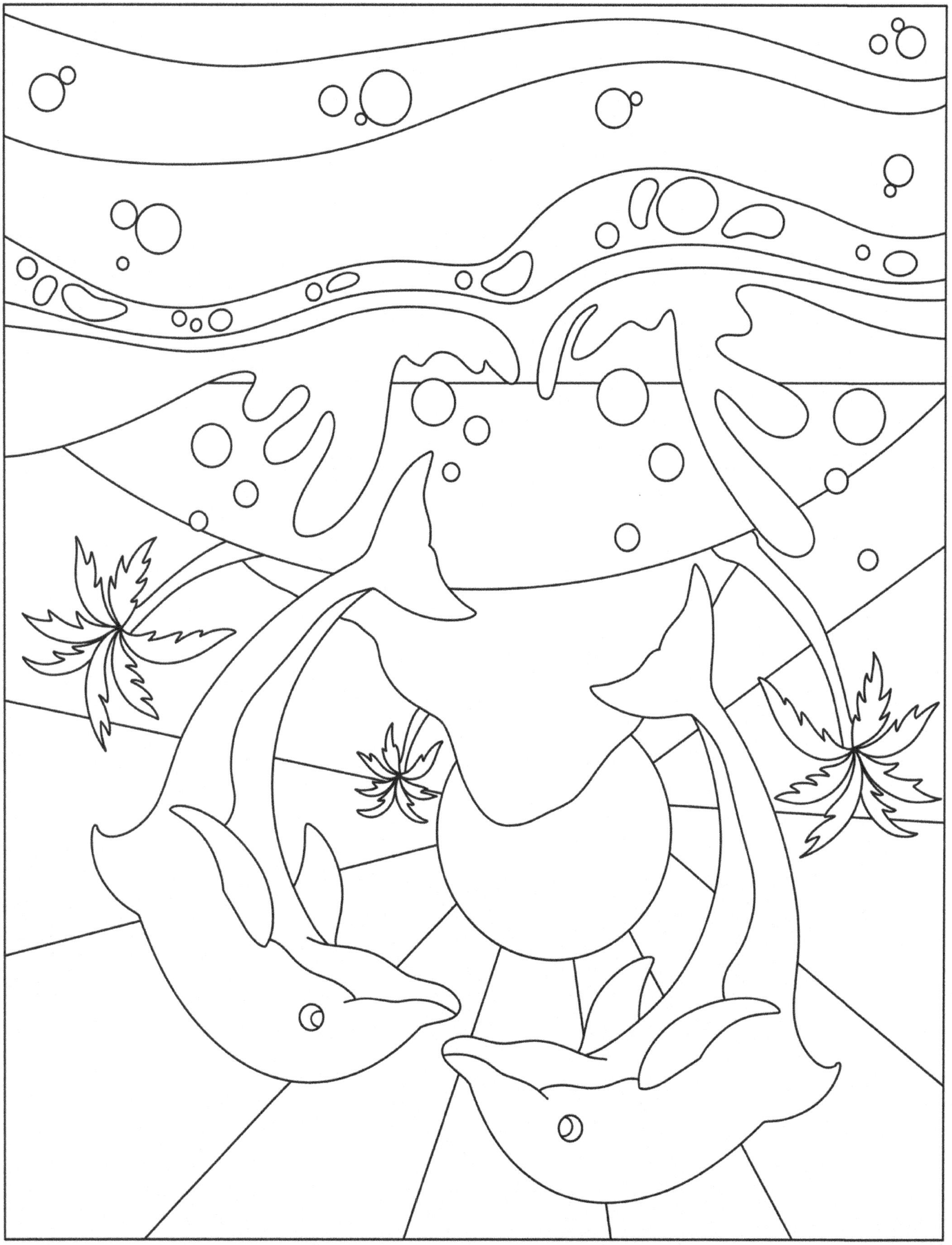

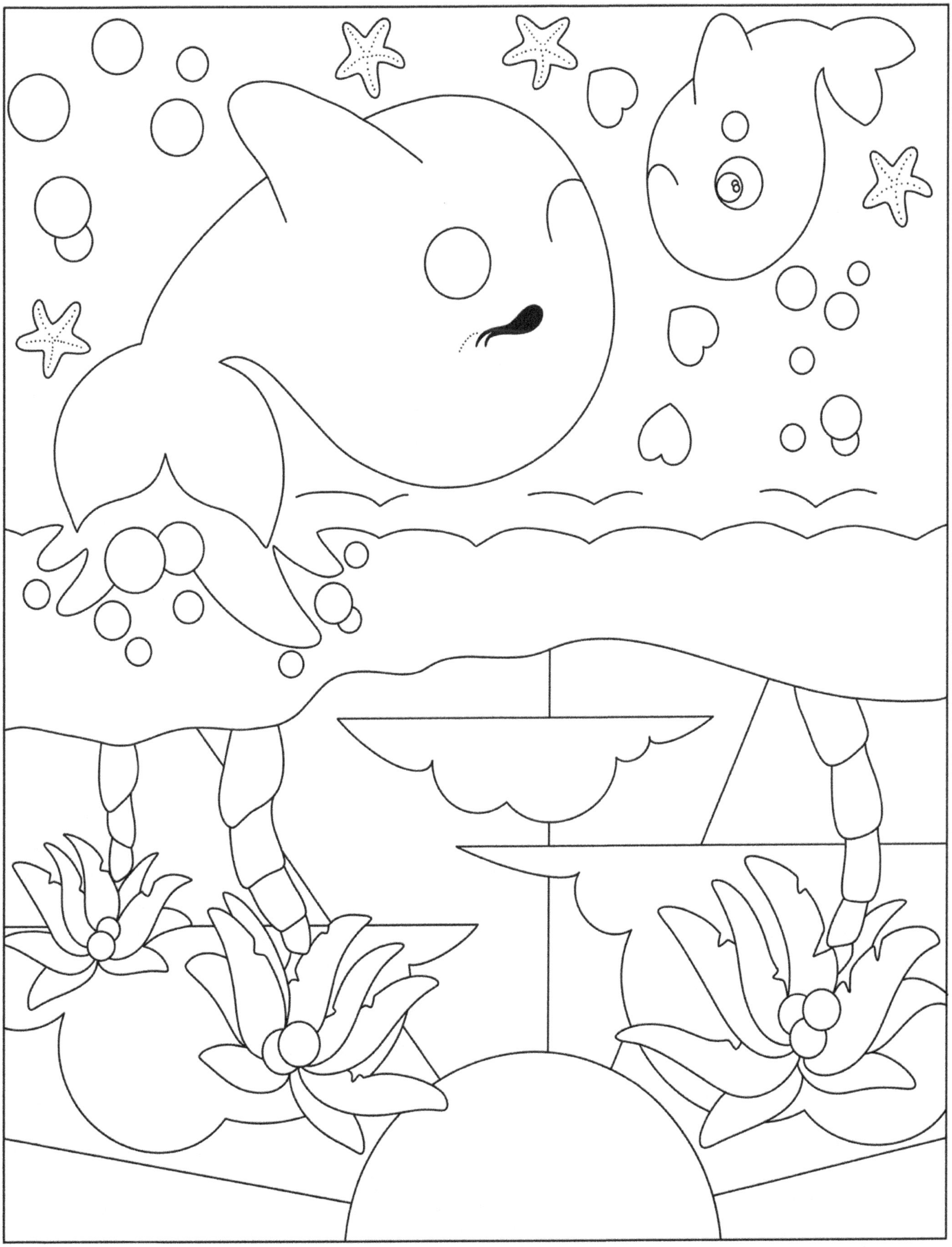

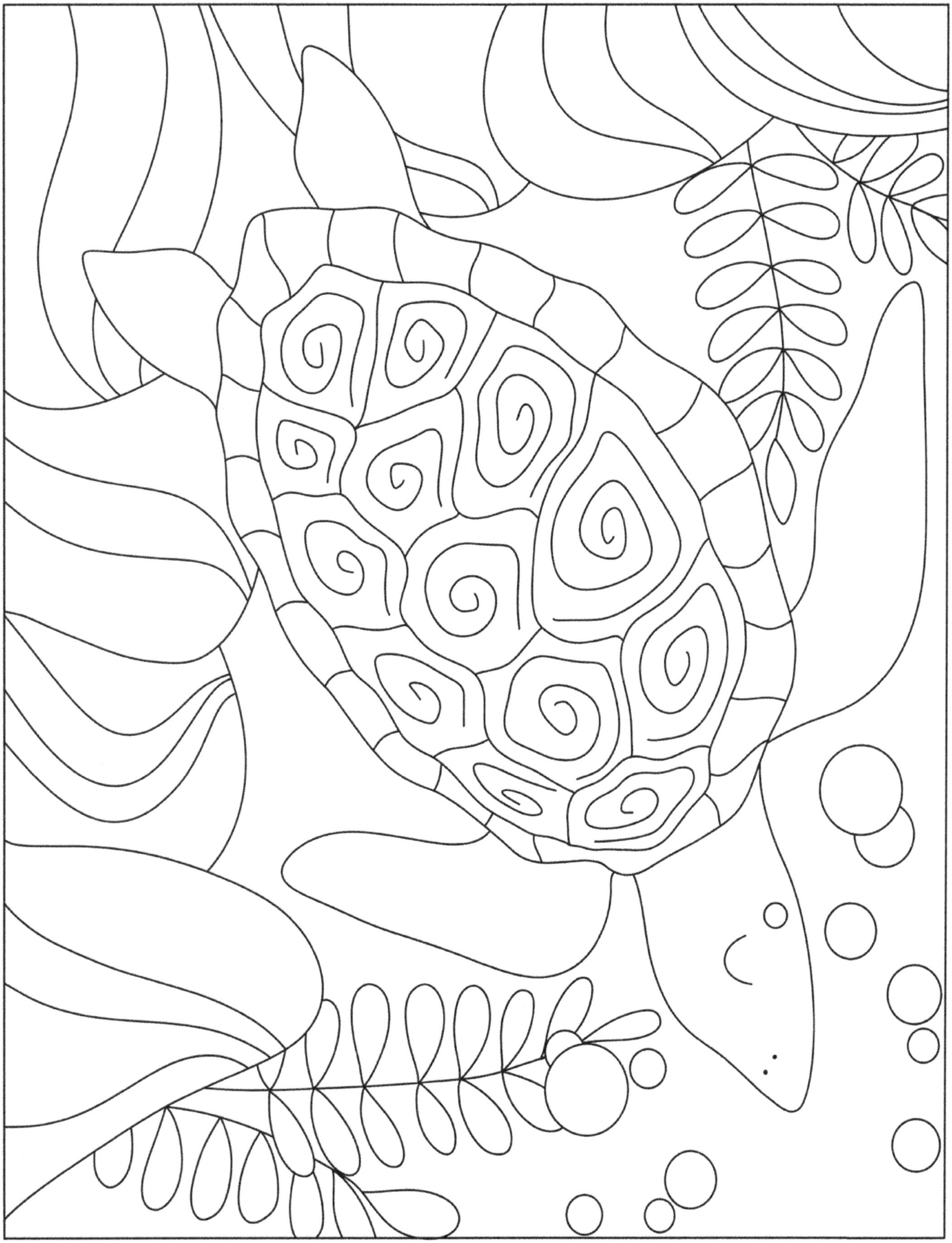

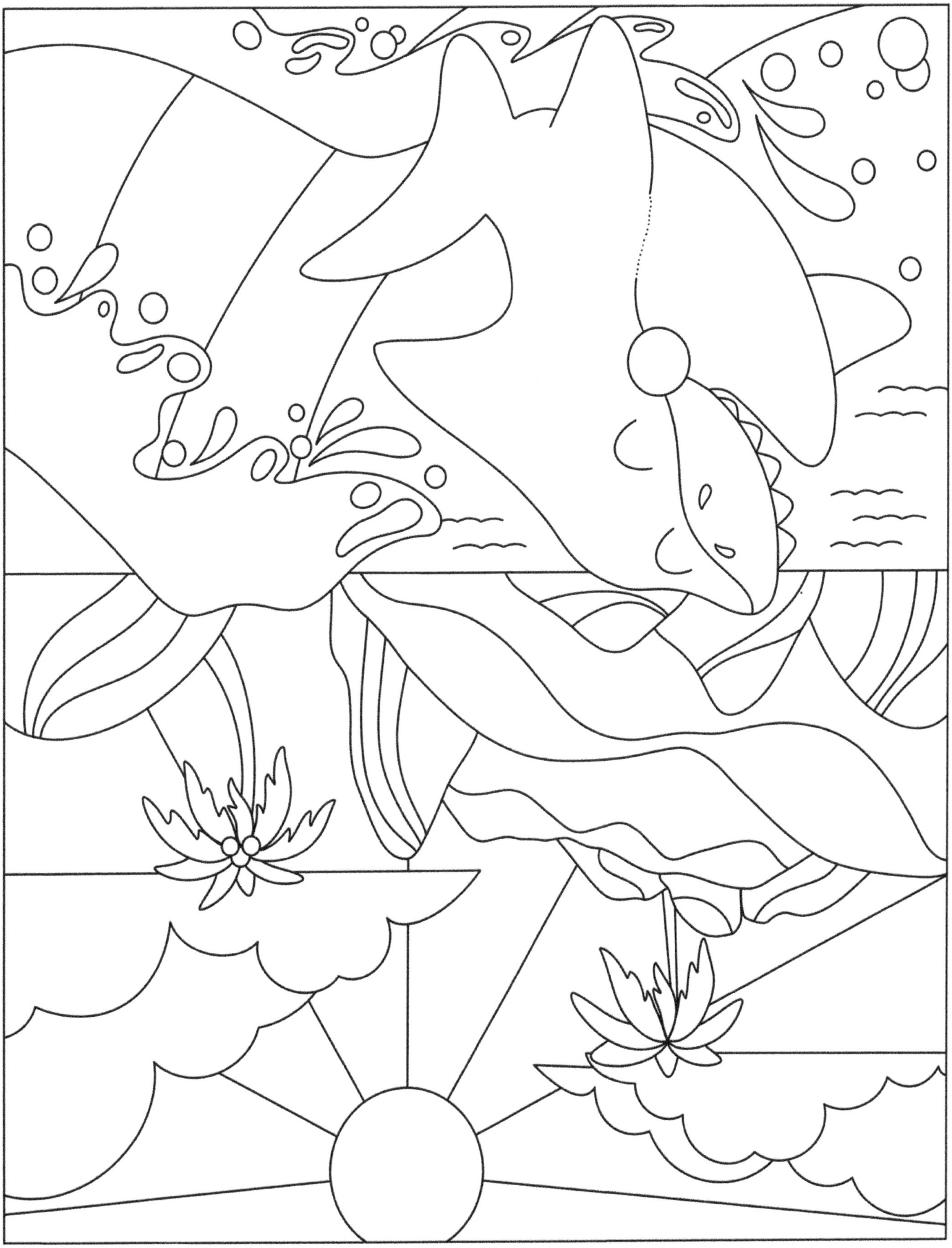

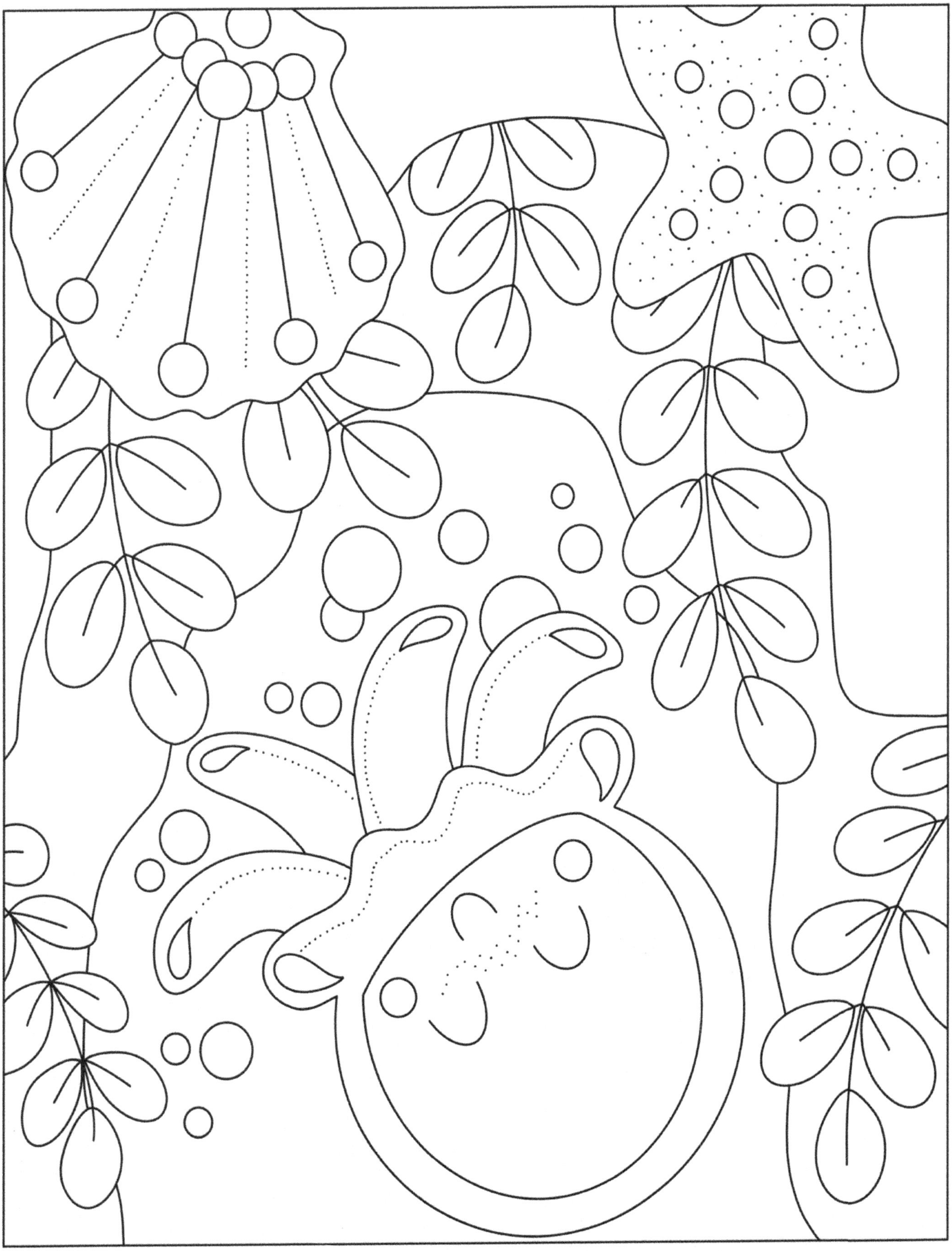

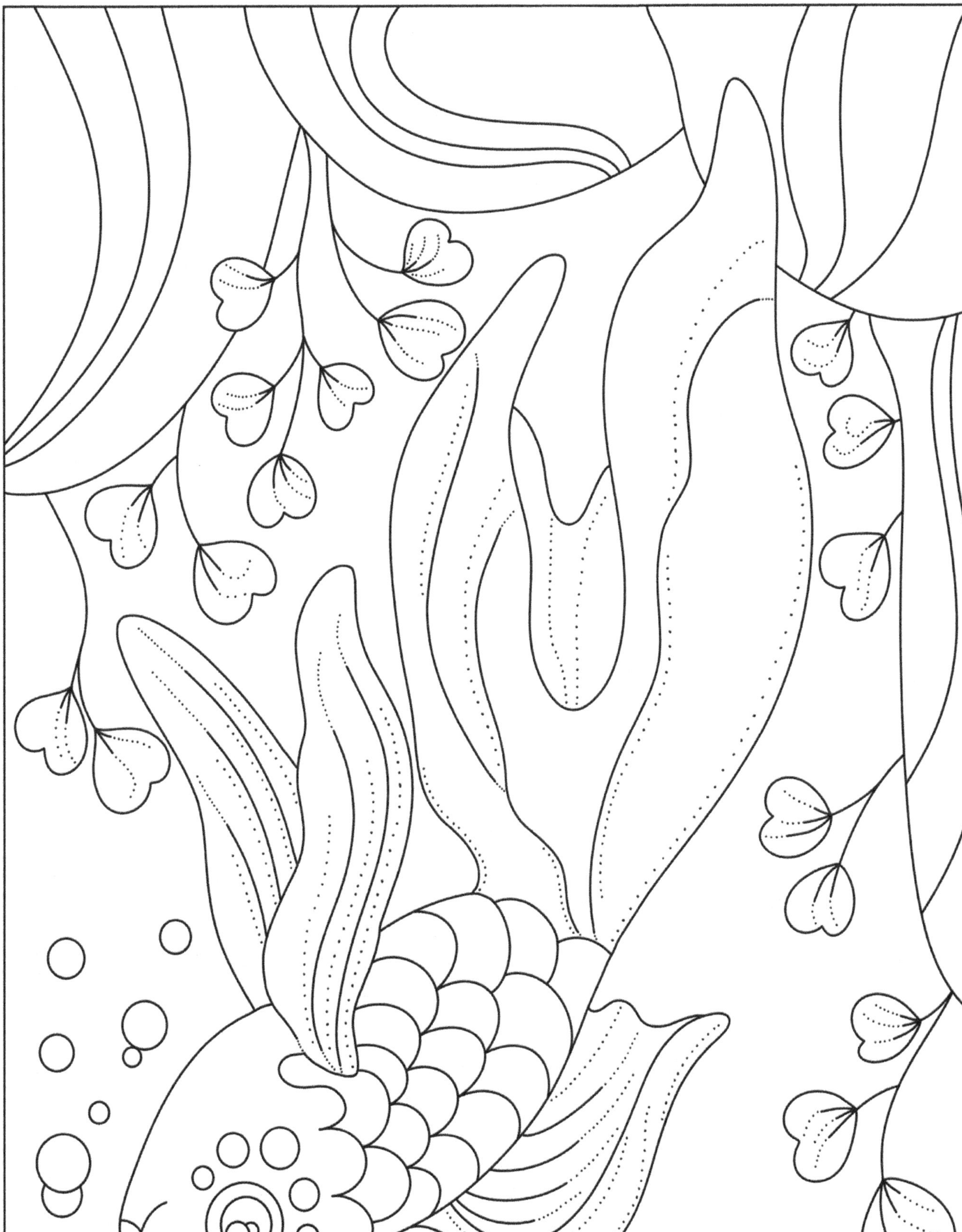

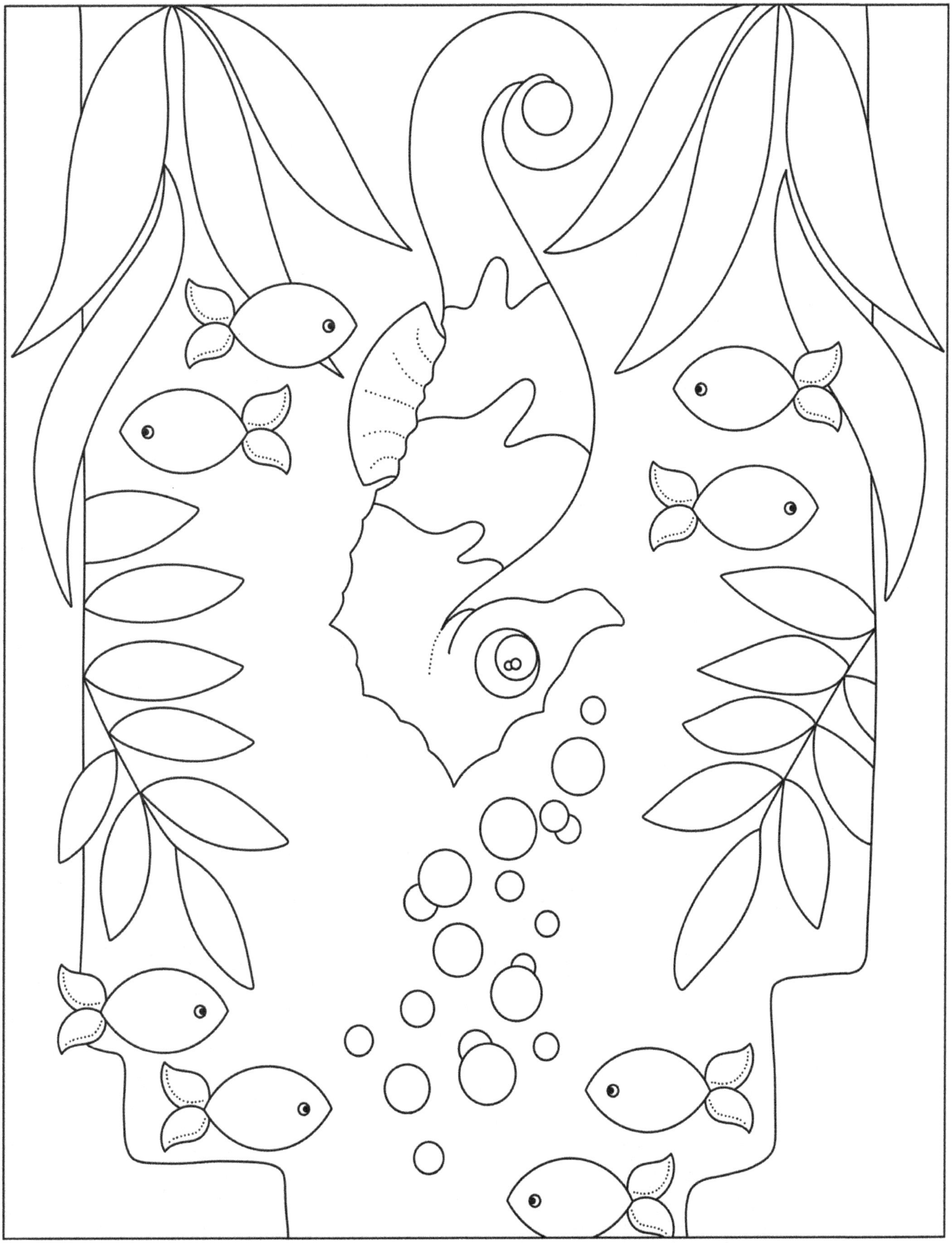

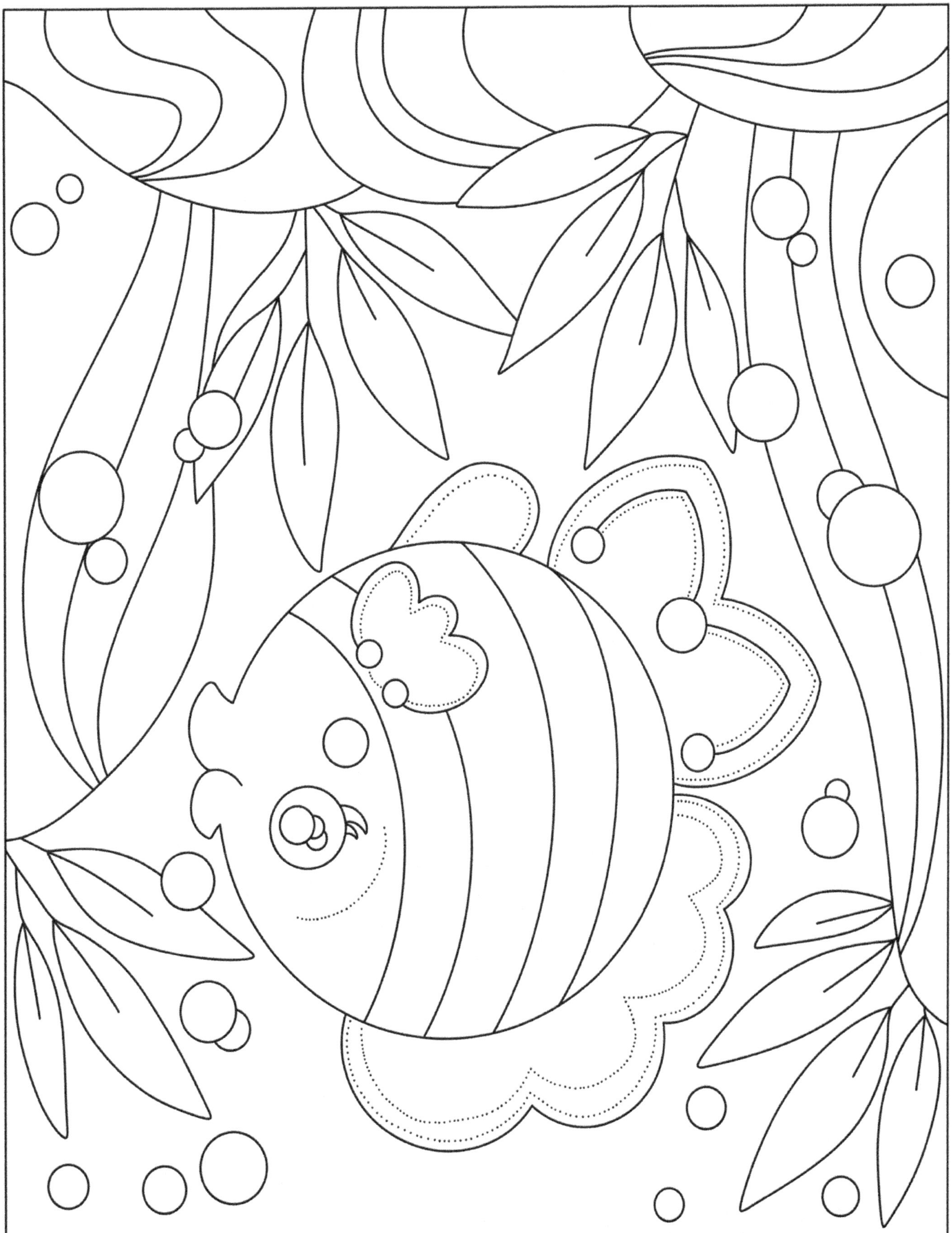

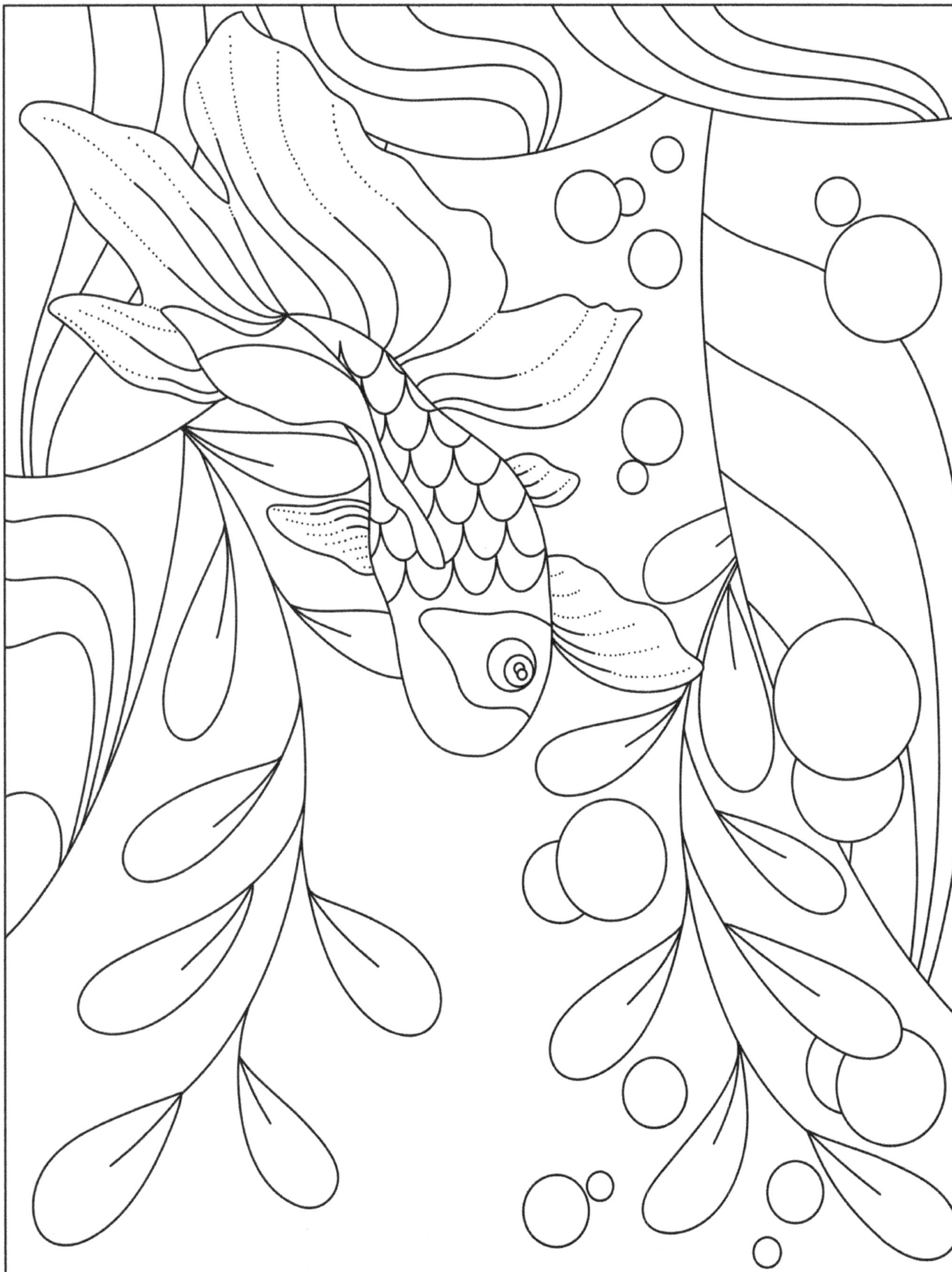

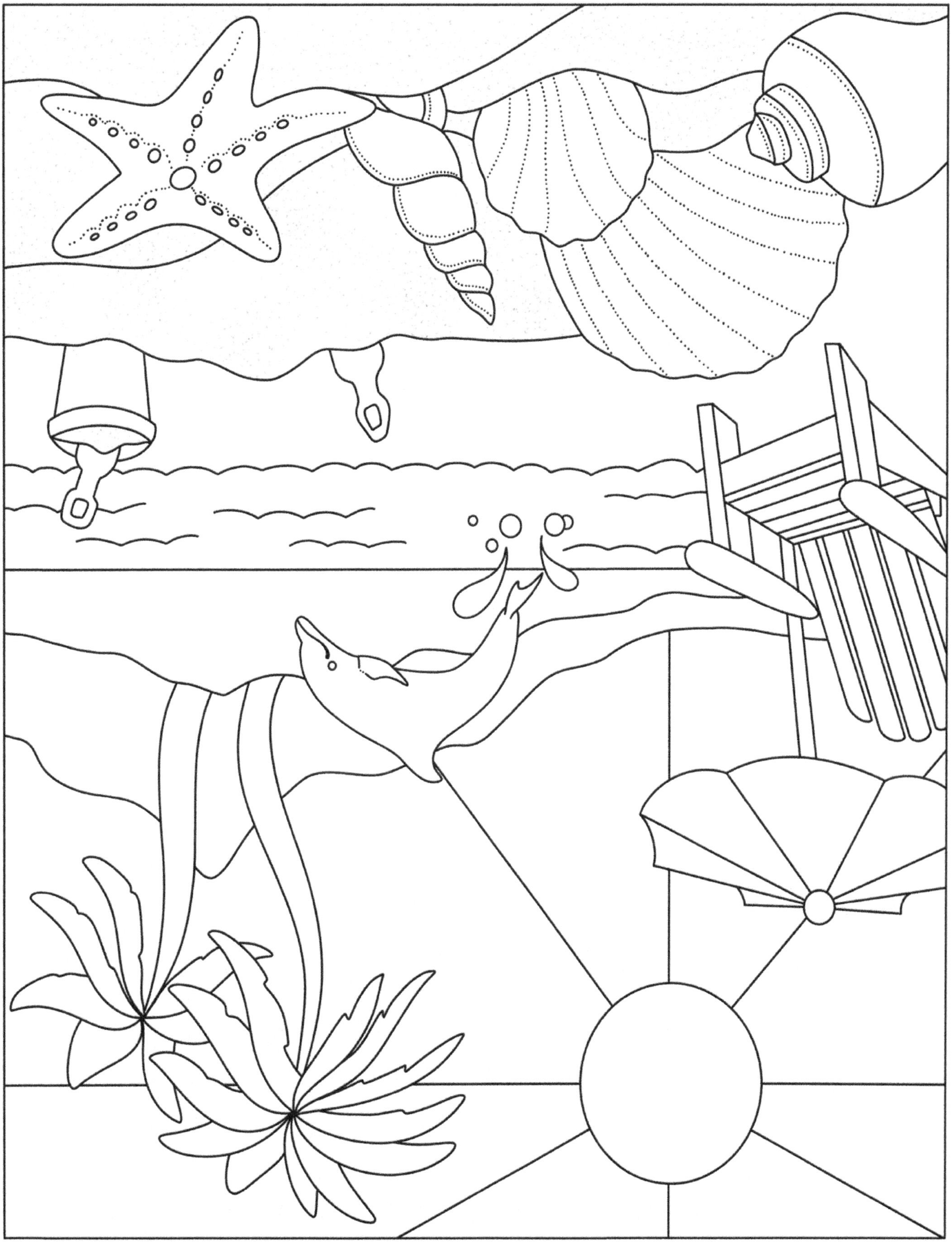

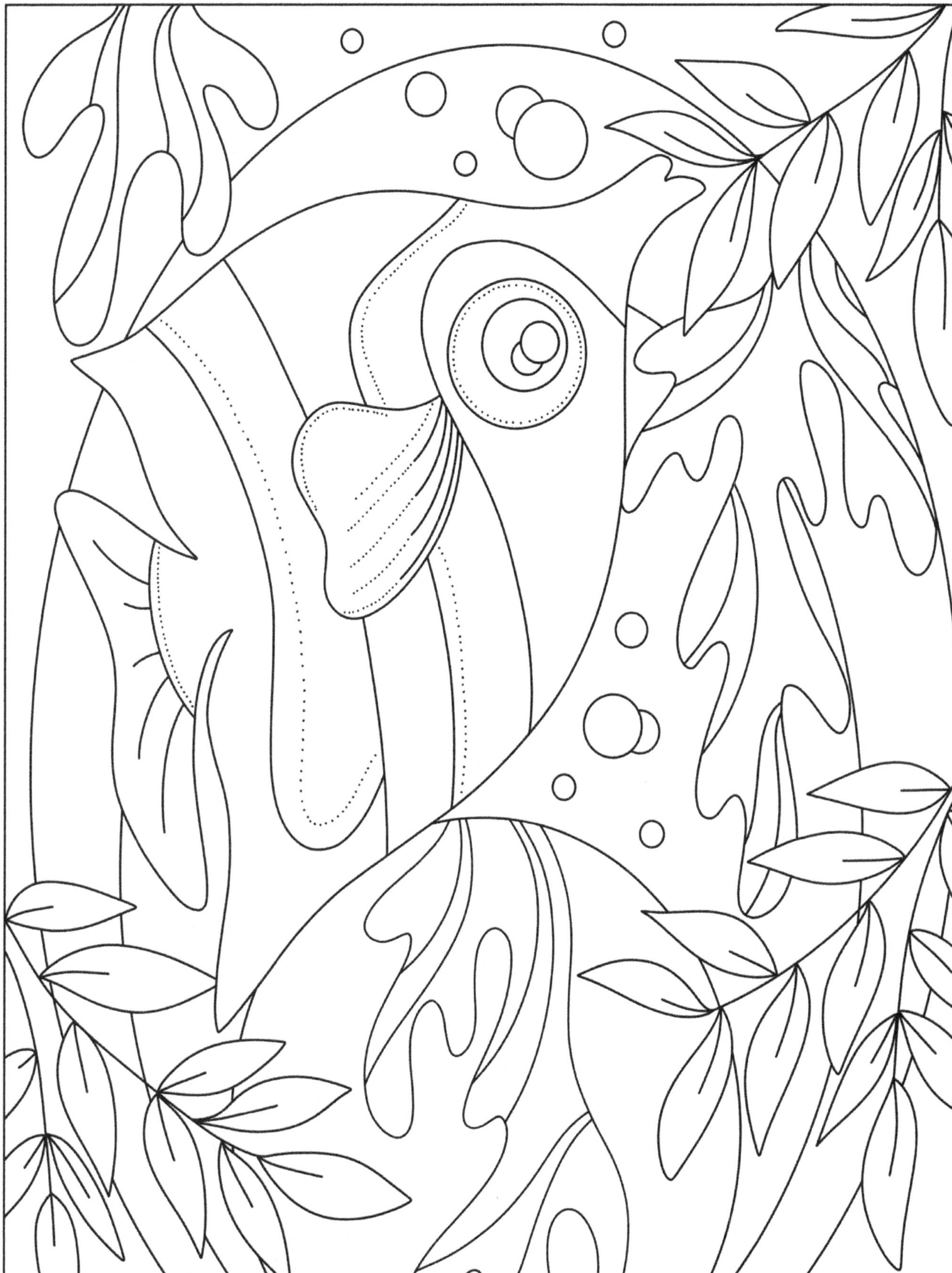

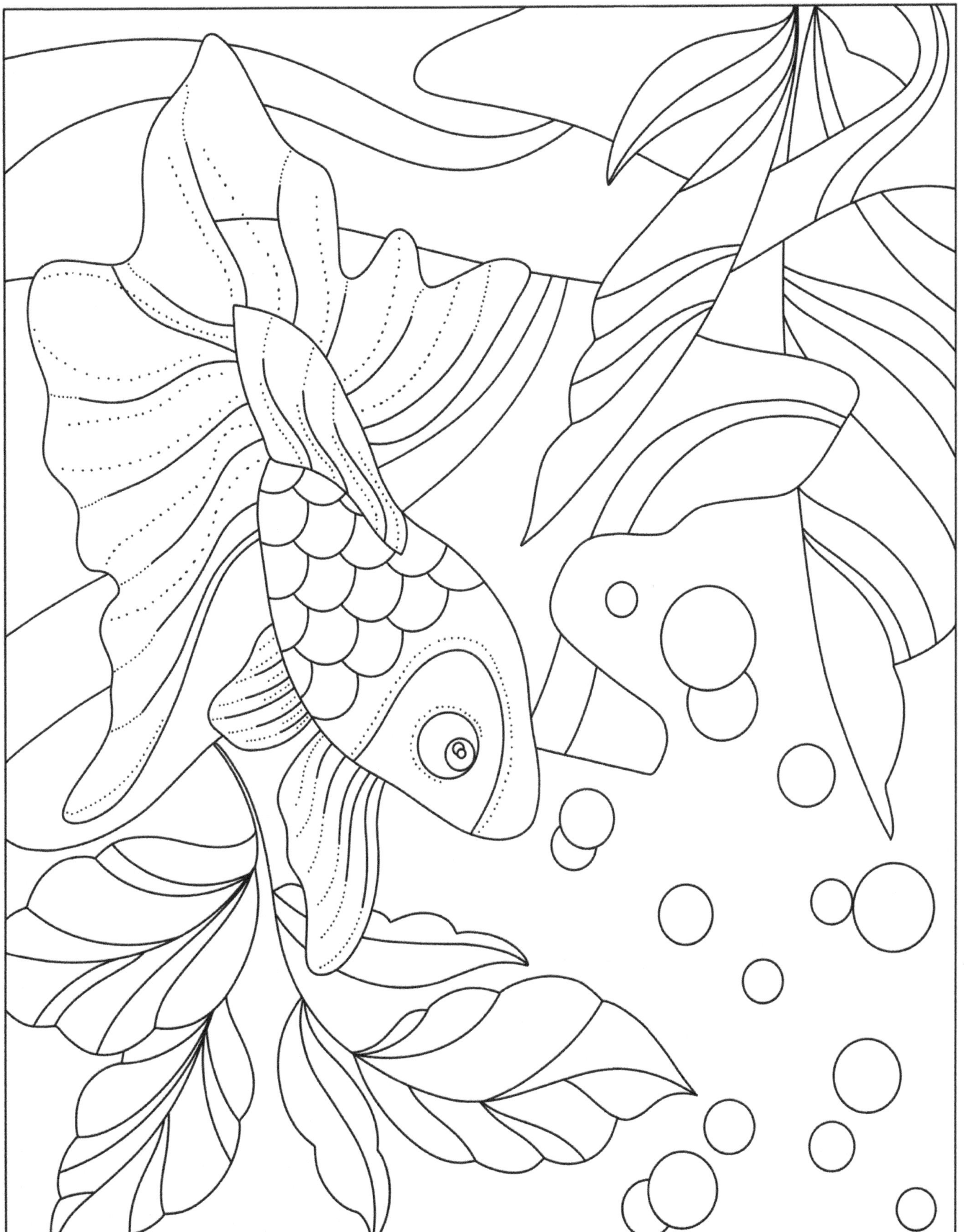

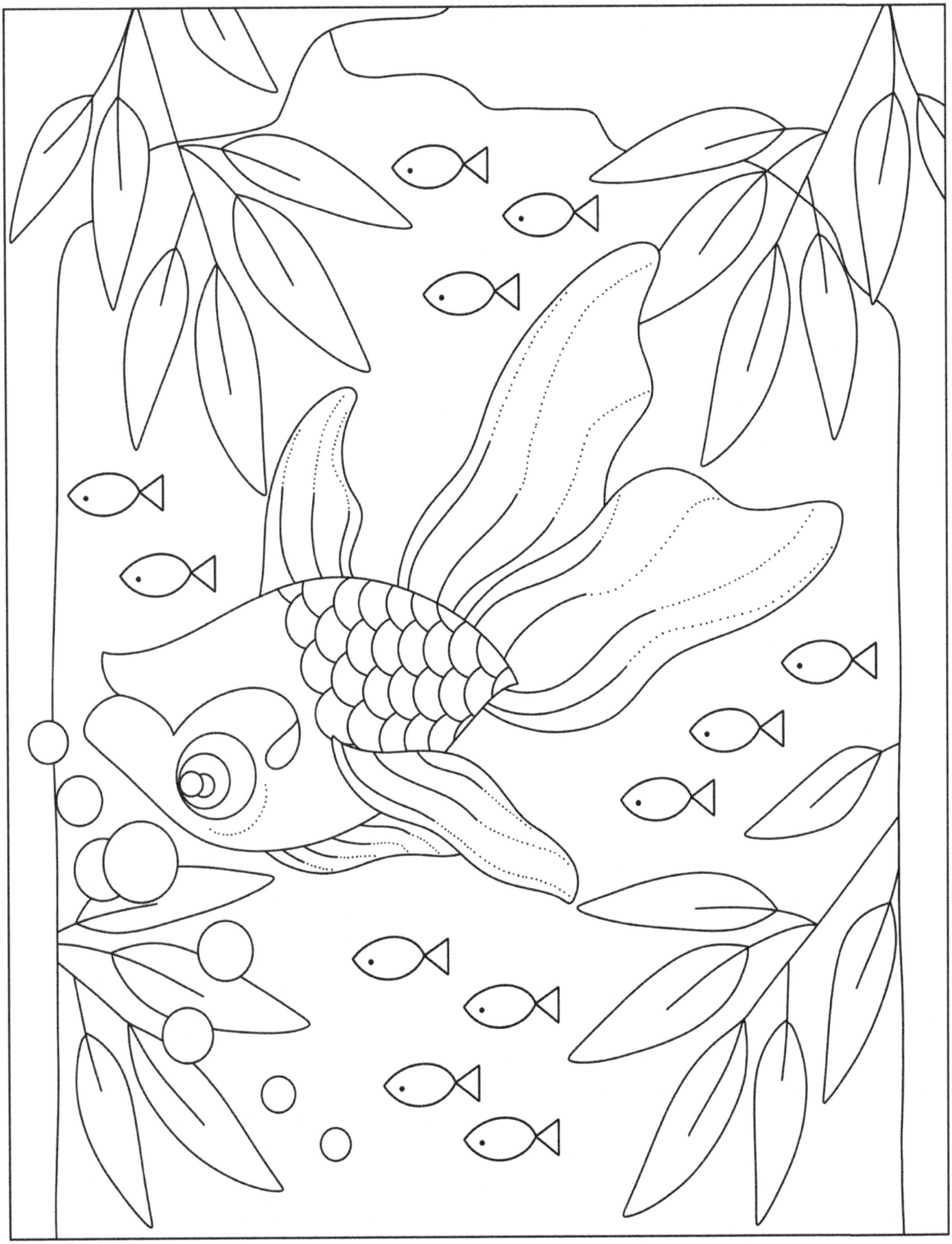

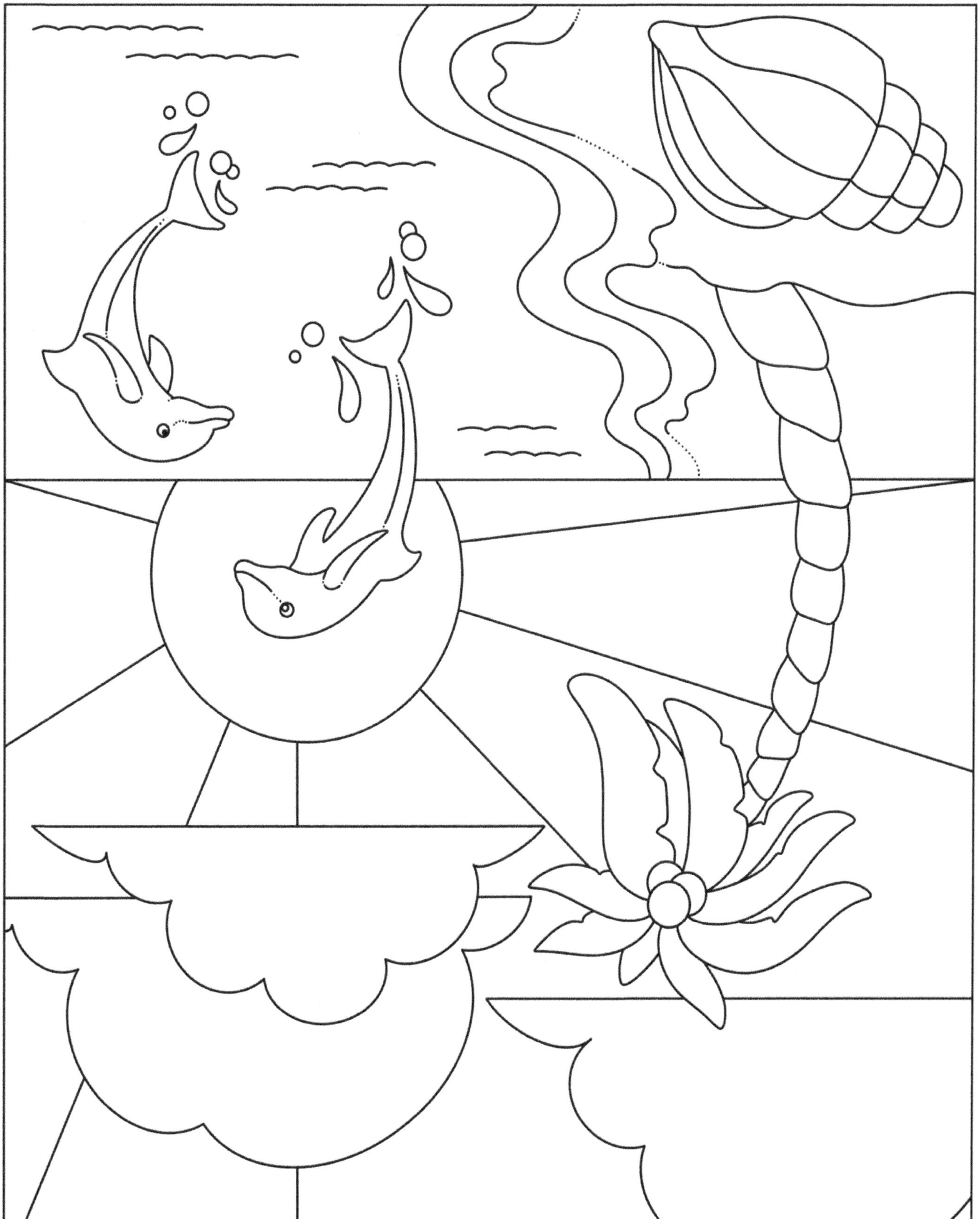

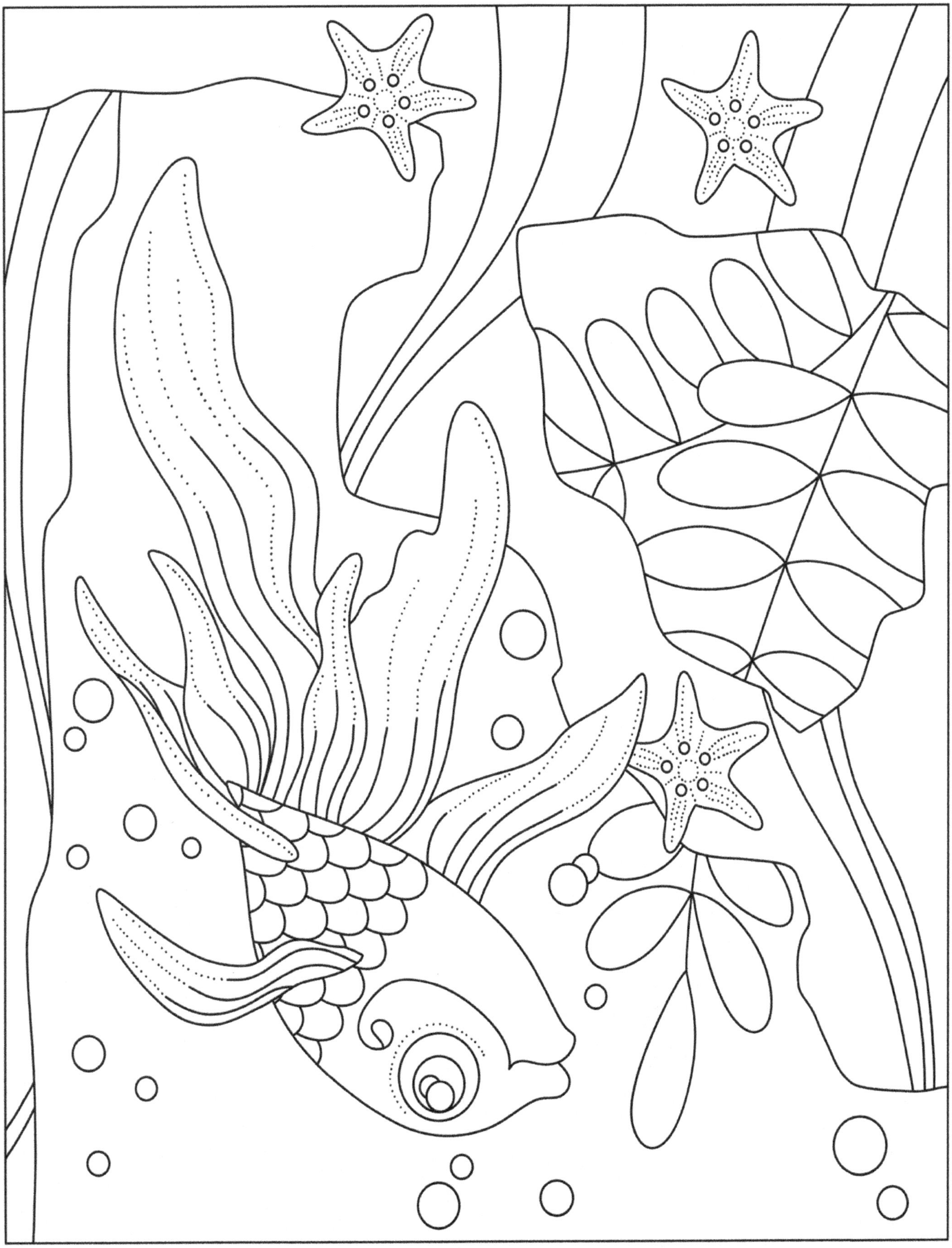

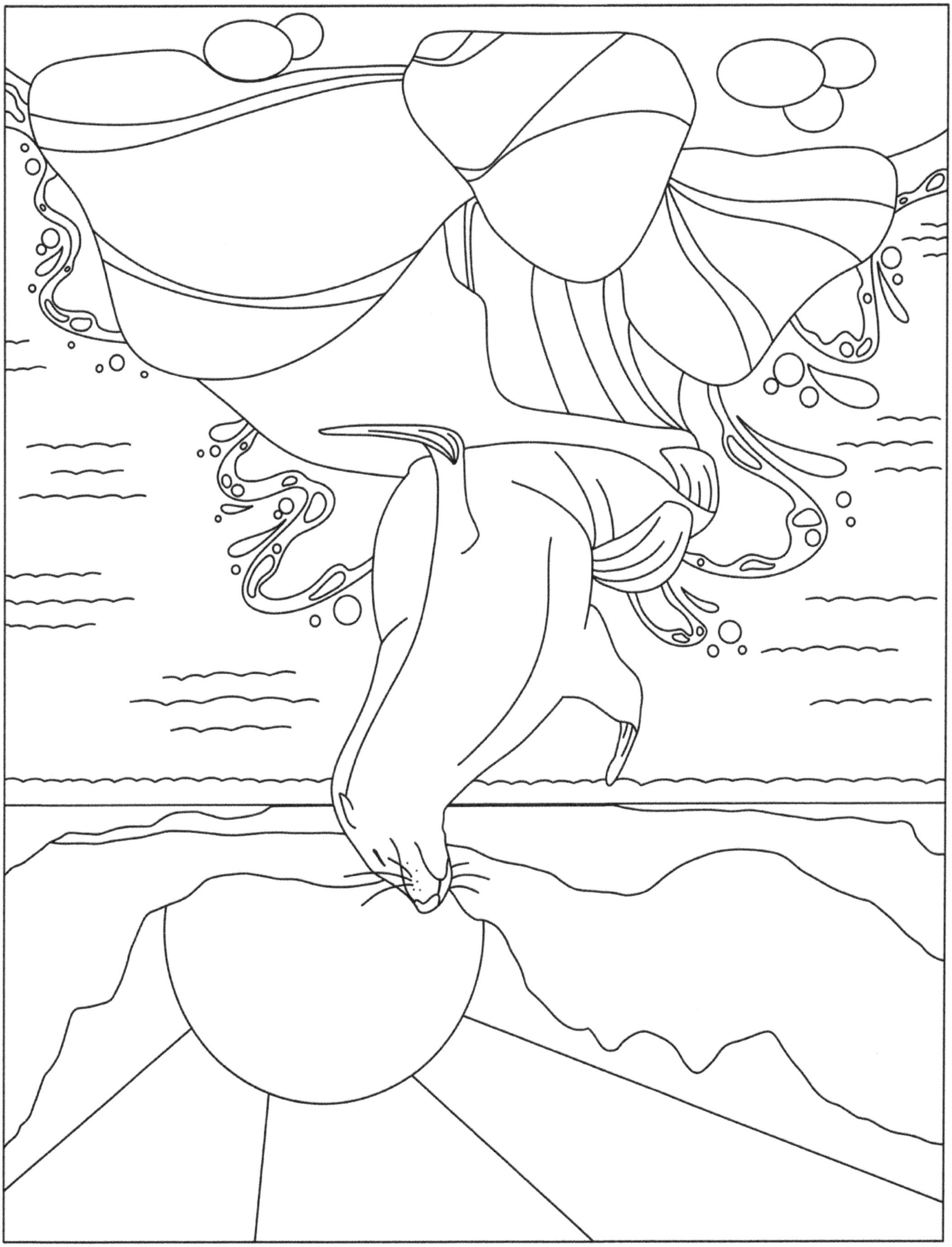

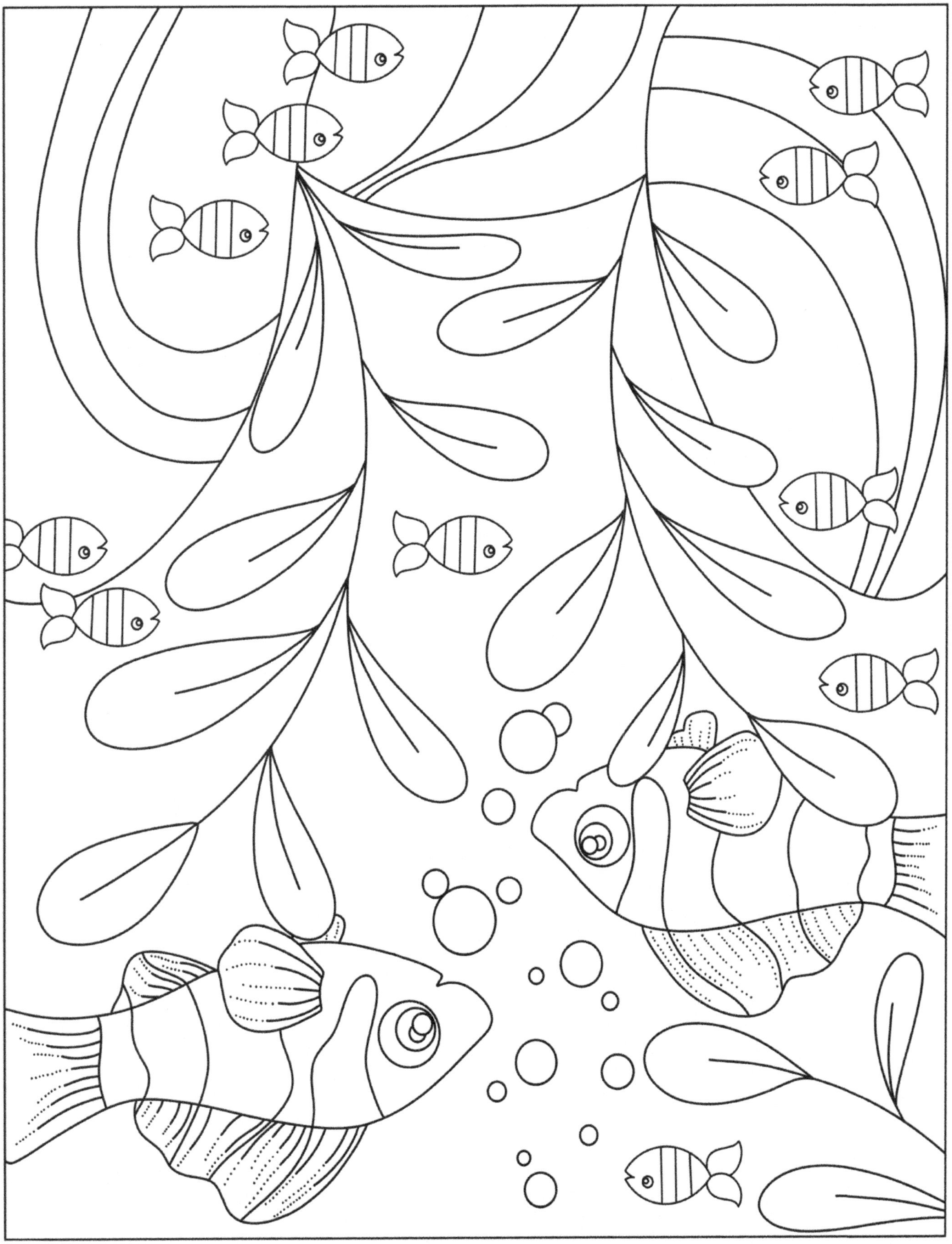

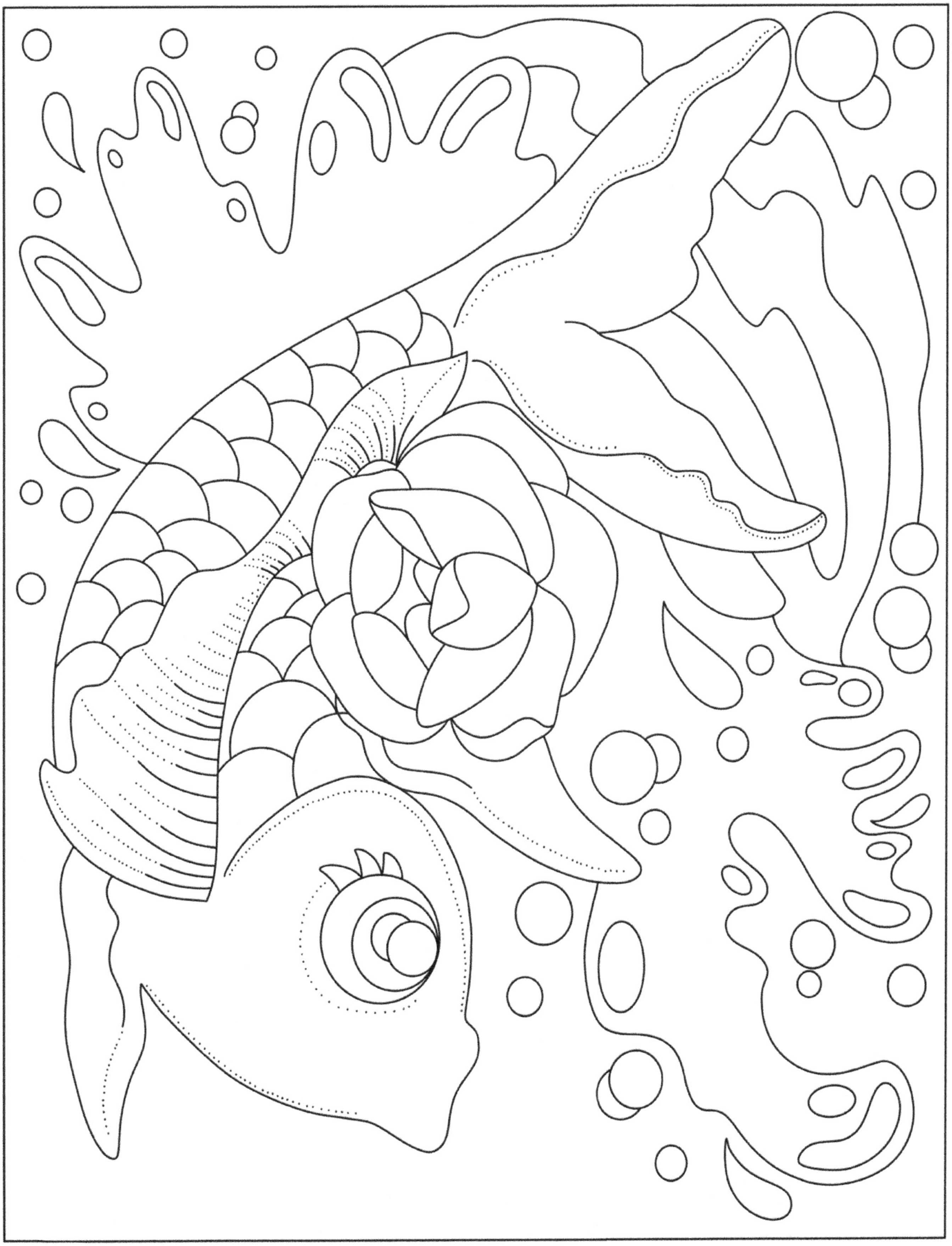

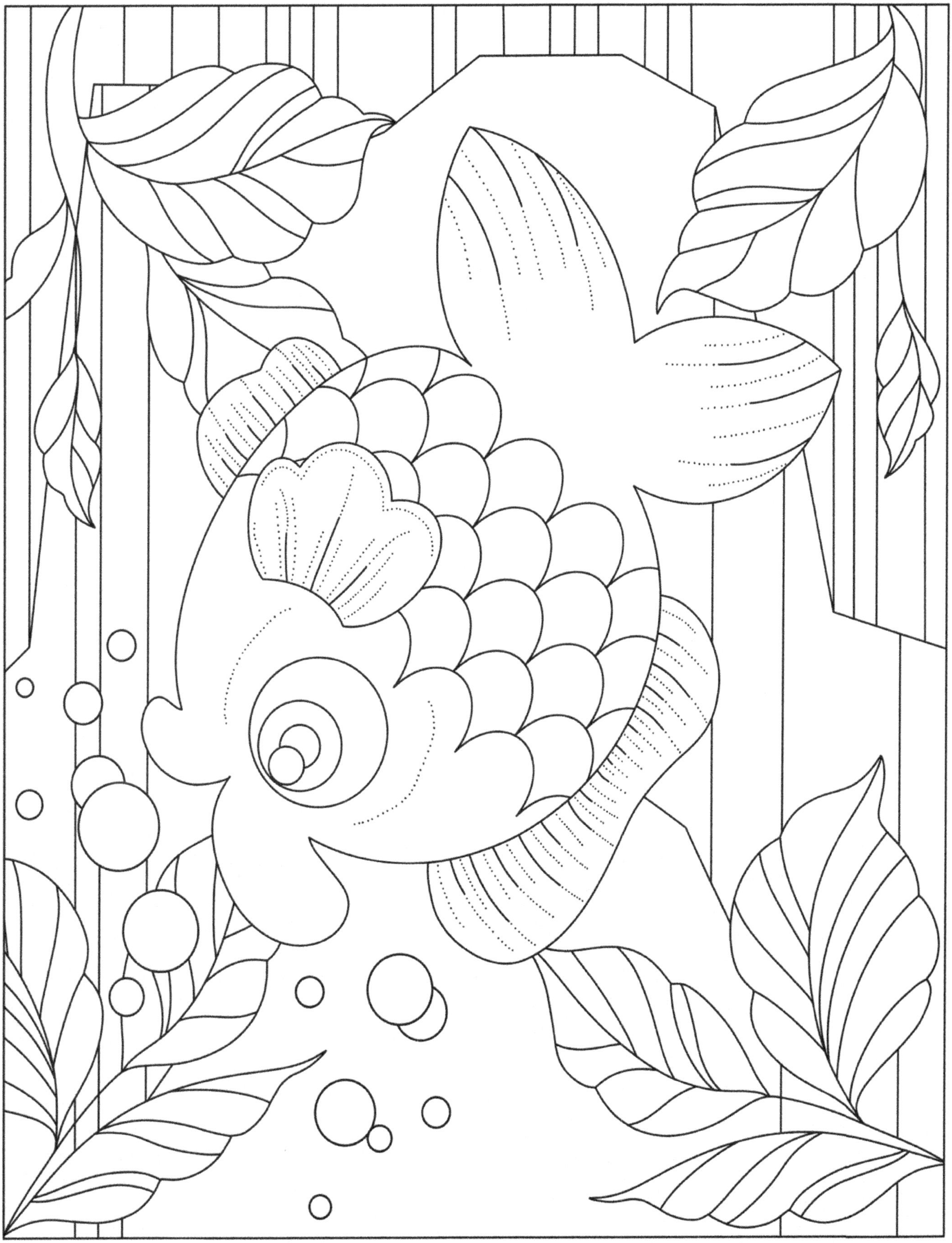

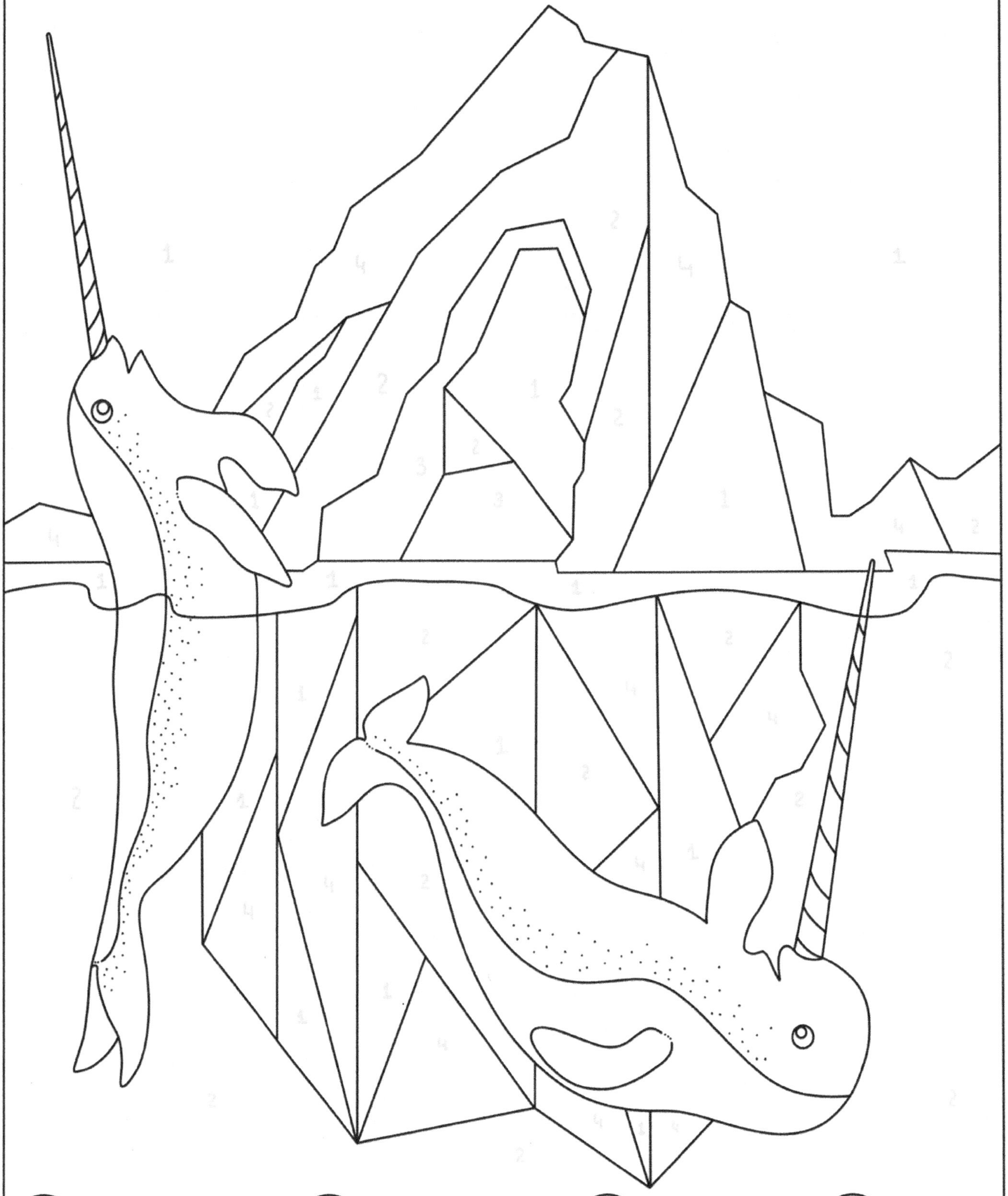

1 Light Blue

2 Dark Blue

3 Green

4 Gray

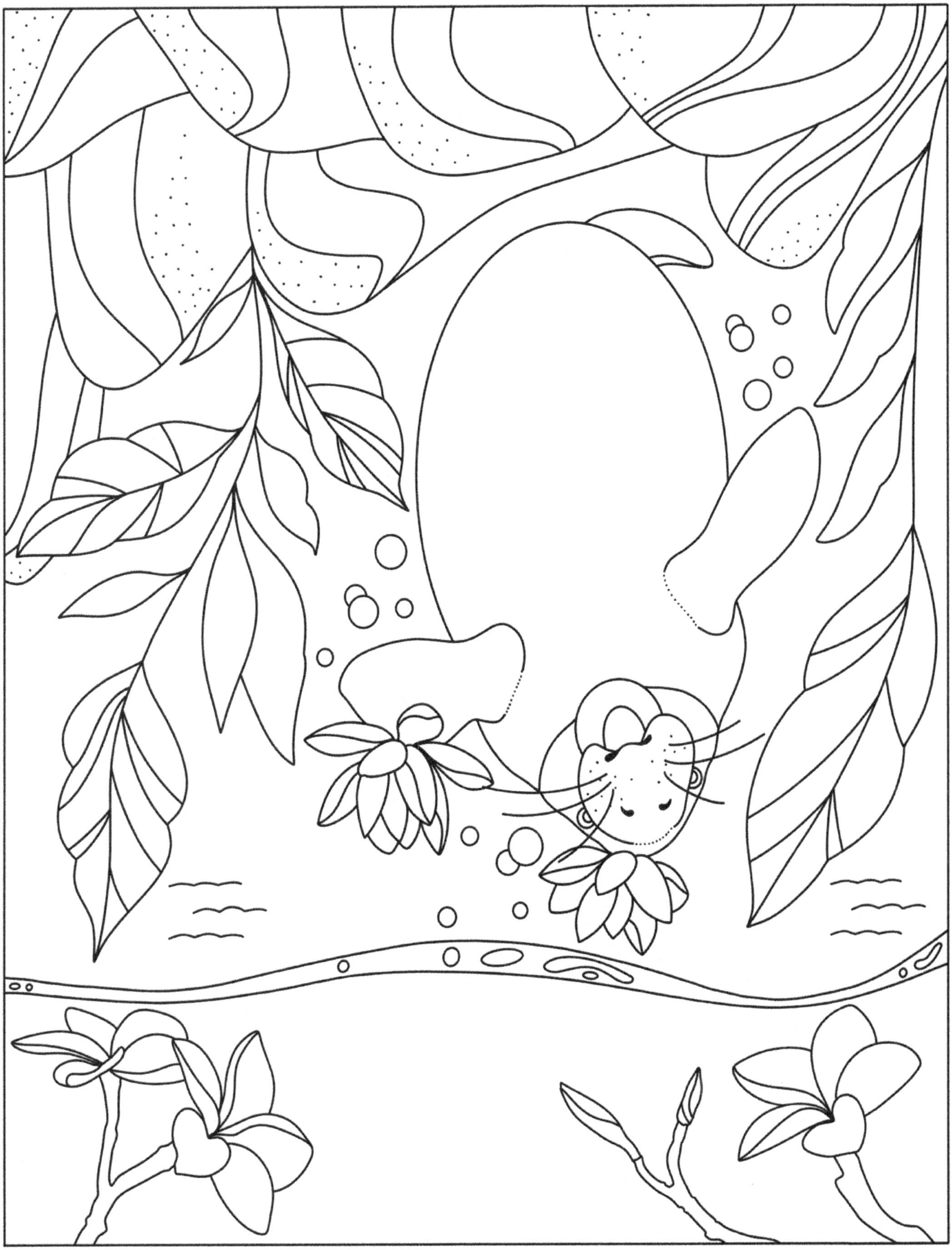

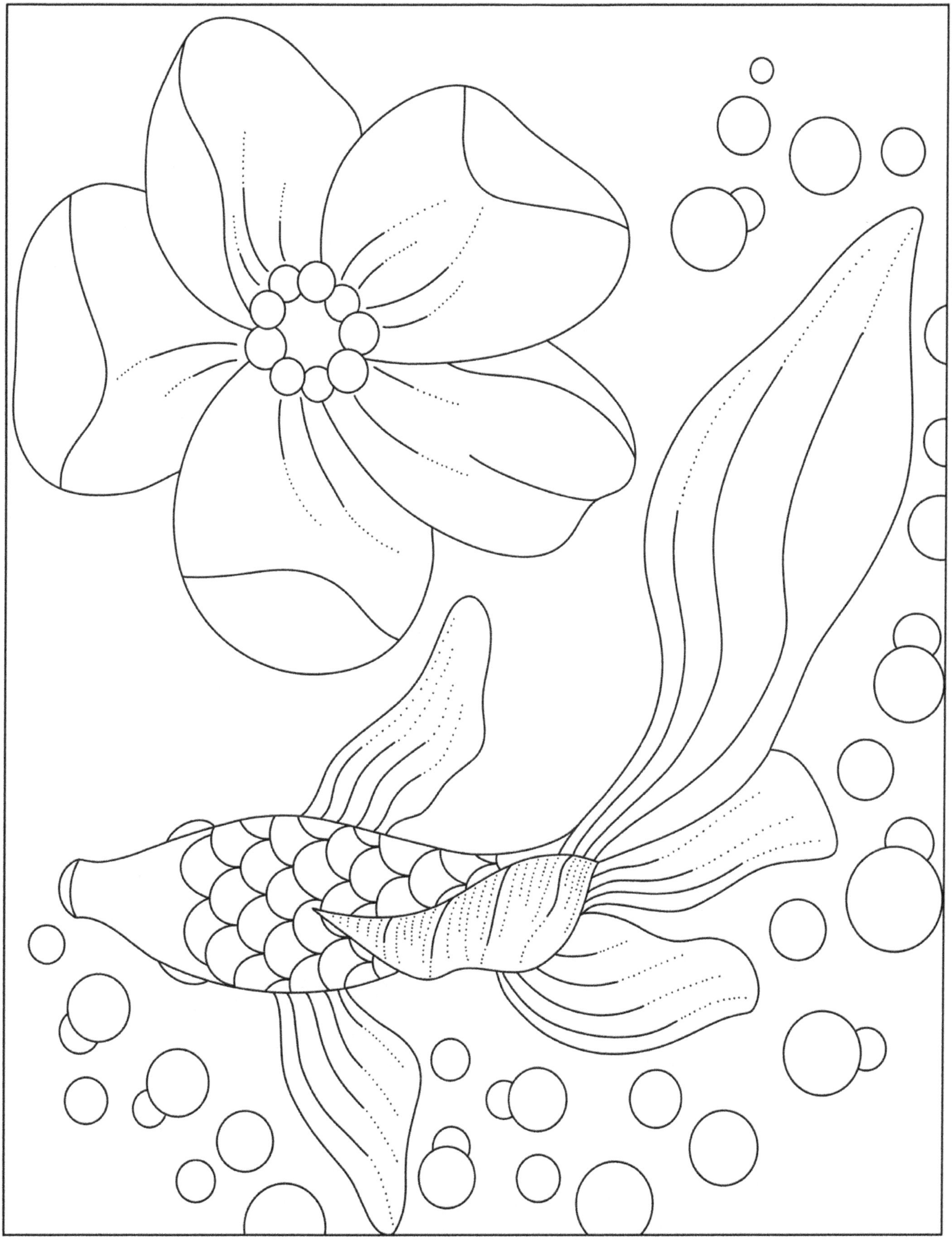

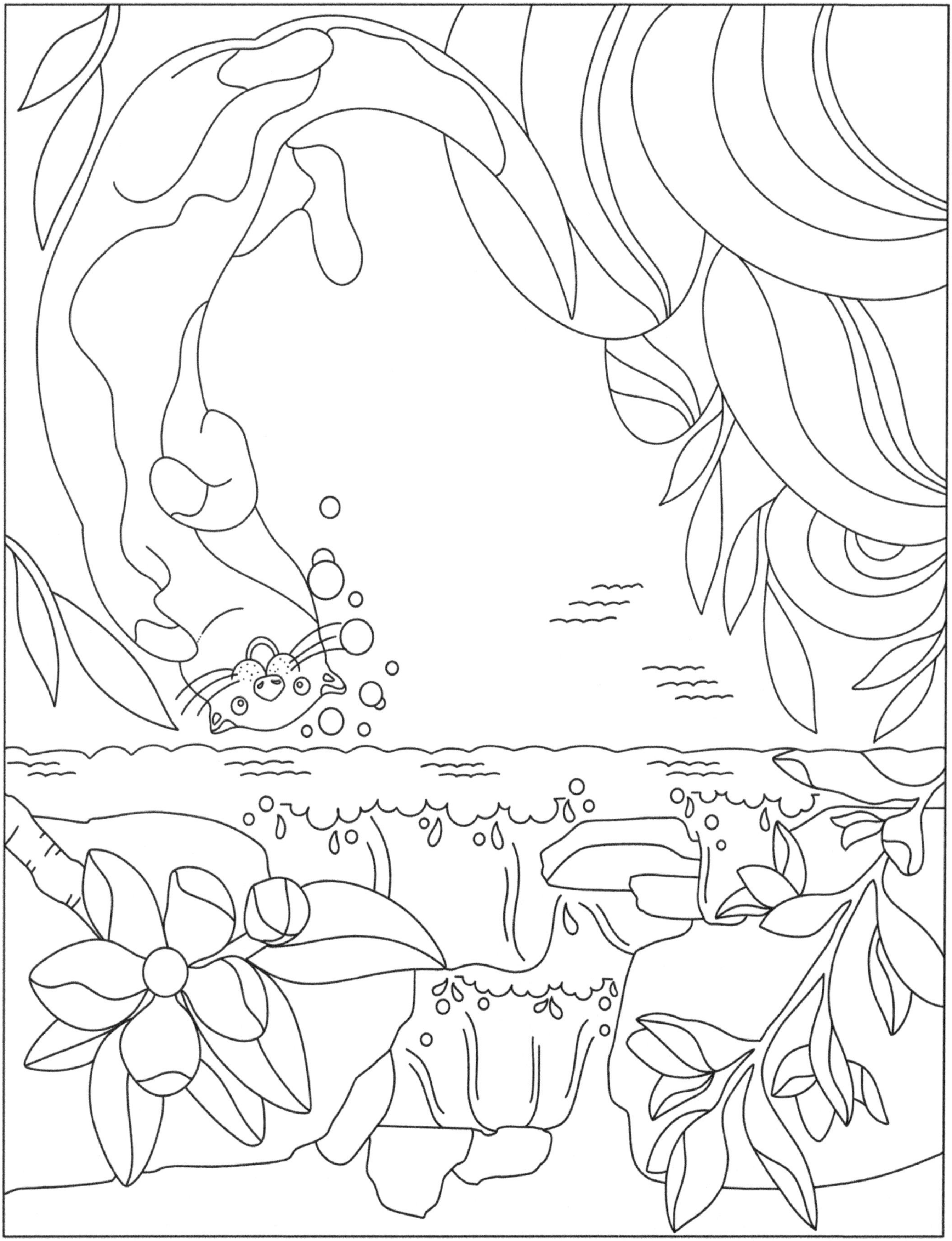

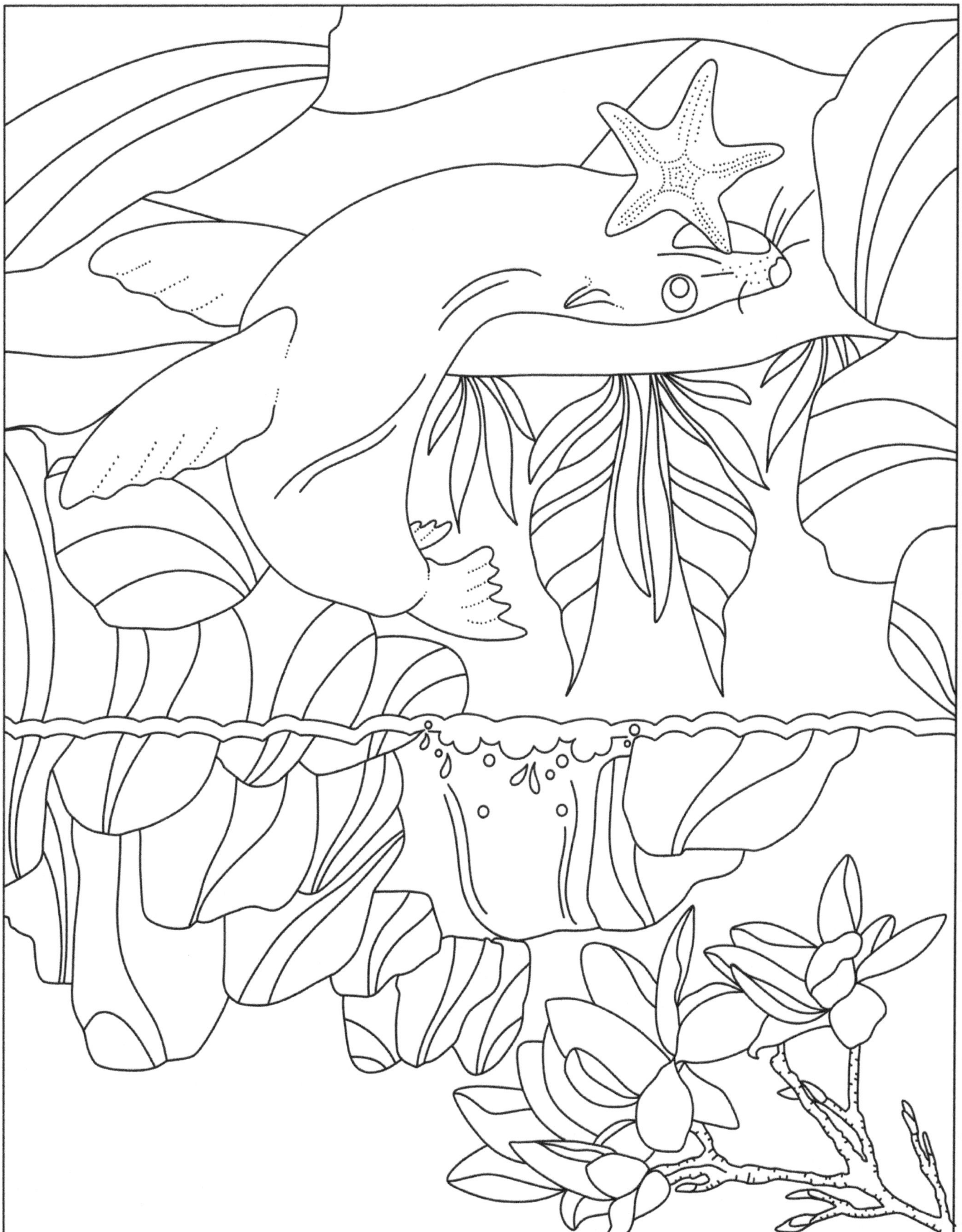

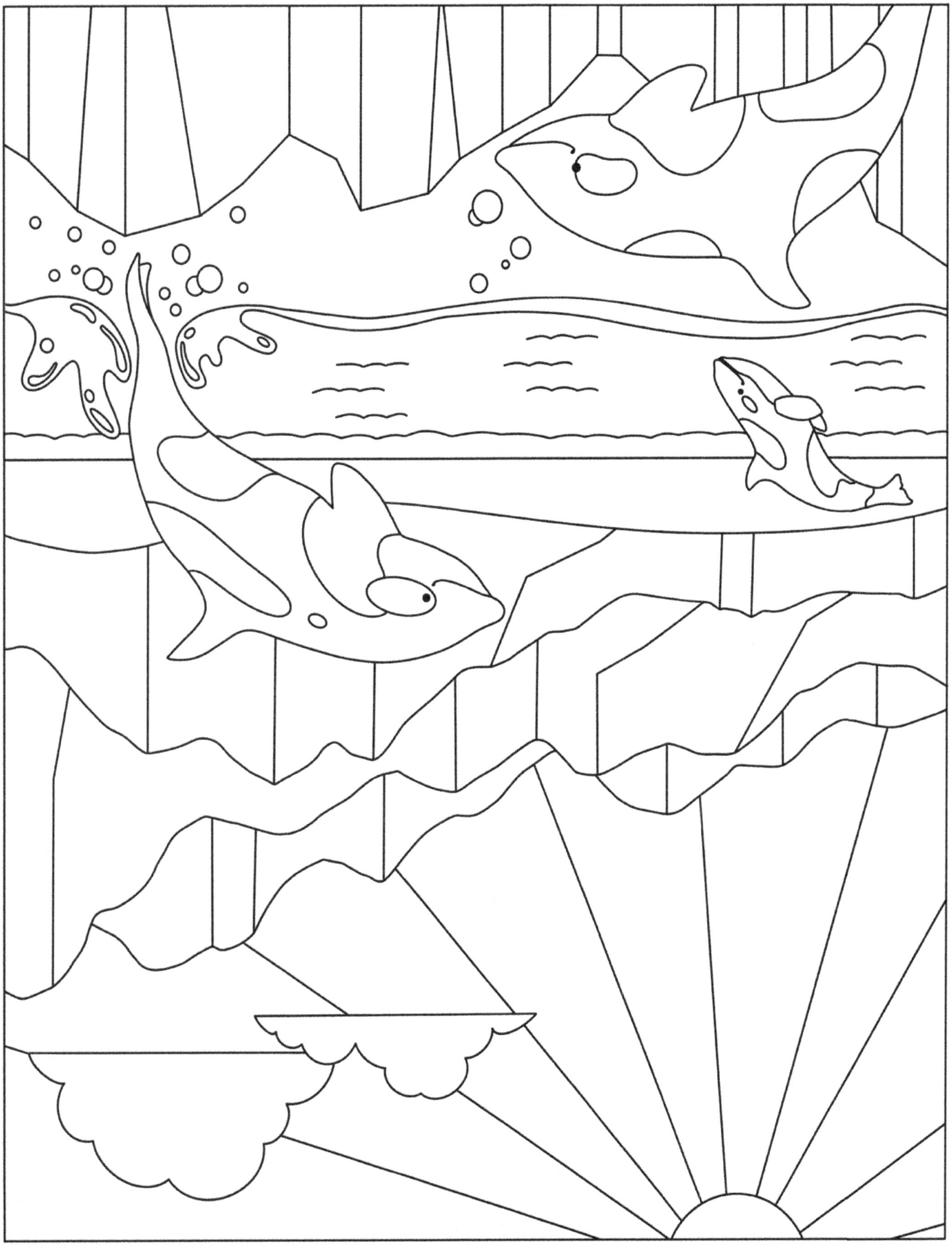

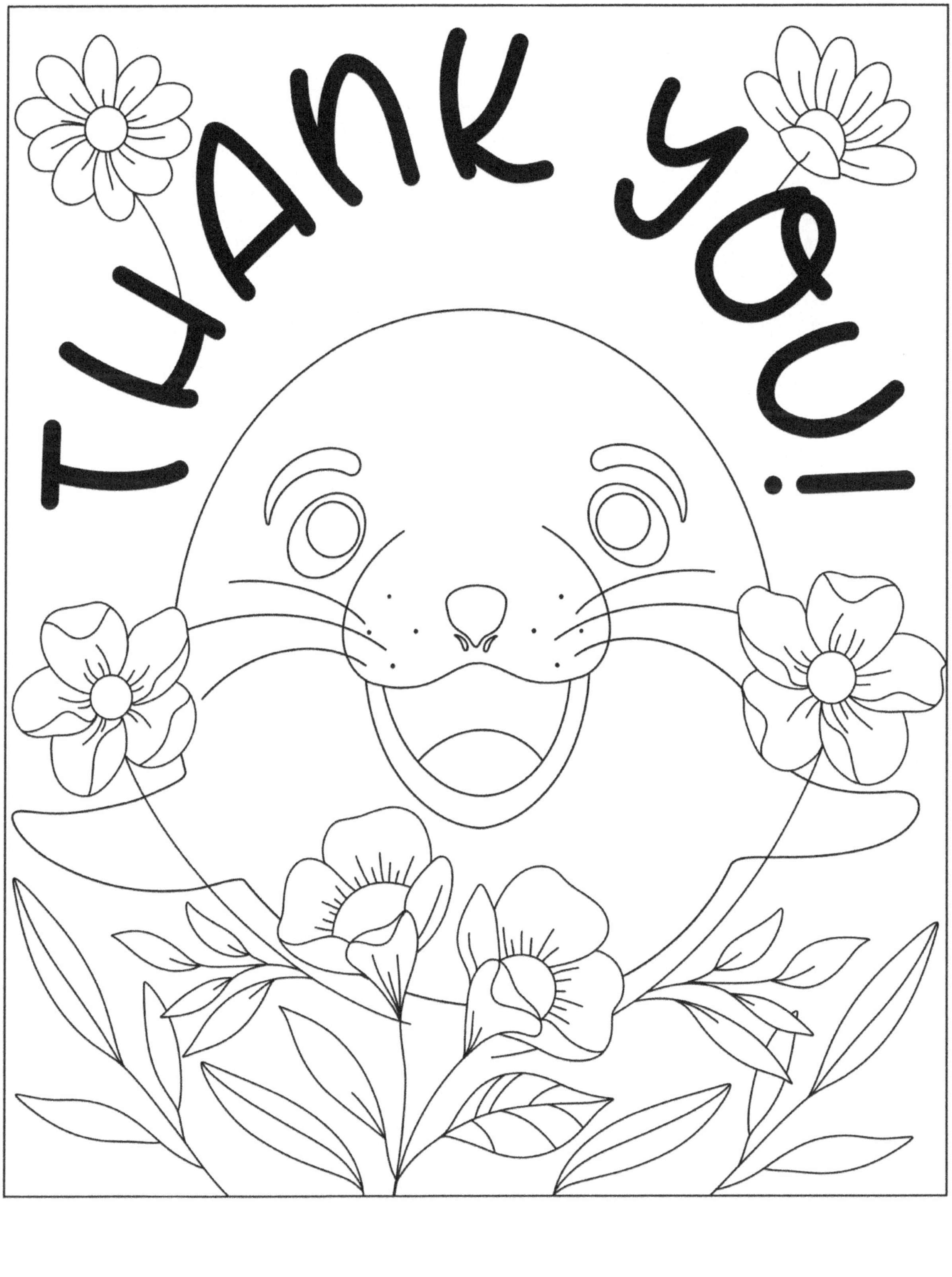
THANK YOU!

Made in the USA
Las Vegas, NV
07 May 2022

48533305R00037